We're from
Australia

Victoria Parker

Welcome to Australia!

Heinemann
LIBRARY

Young Explorer

www.heinemann.co.uk/library
Visit our website to find out more information about **Heinemann Library** books.

To order:
☎ Phone 44 (0) 1865 888066
▤ Send a fax to 44 (0) 1865 314091
▣ Visit the Heinemann Bookshop at www.heinemann.co.uk/library to browse our catalogue and order online.

First published in Great Britain by Heinemann Library, Halley Court, Jordan Hill, Oxford OX2 8EJ, part of Harcourt Education.
Heinemann is a registered trademark of Harcourt Education Ltd.

Editorial: Jilly Attwood, Kate Bellamy and Catherine Williams
Design: Ron Kamen and Celia Jones
Photographer: Martin Brent
Picture Research: Maria Joannou
Production: Séverine Ribierre

Originated by Ambassador Litho Ltd
Printed and bound in China by South China Printing Company

10 digit ISBN 0 431 11935 X
13 digit ISBN 978 0 431 11935 9
09 08 07 06
10 9 8 7 6 5 4 3 2

British Library Cataloguing in Publication Data

Parker, Victoria
We're From Australia
994'. 07

A full catalogue record for this book is available from the British Library.

Acknowledgements
Martin Brent pp. 1, 5a, 5b, 6, 7, 8, 9a, 9b, 10a, 10b, 11, 12, 13a, 13b, 14, 15a, 15b, 16, 17a, 17b, 18a, 18b, 20, 21, 22, 23, 24a, 24b, 25a, 25b, 26, 27a, 27b; Corbis/Royalty Free pp. 4a, 4b, 5b, 5c, 28a, 28b, 29; Corbis/Robert Garvey p. 19

Cover photograph of Dylan and his friends, reproduced with permission of Martin Brent.

Many thanks to Carly, Georgia, Dylan and their families.

Every effort has been made to contact copyright holders of any material reproduced in this book. Any omissions will be rectified in subsequent printings if notice is given to the publishers.

The paper used to print this book comes from sustainable resources.

Contents

Words appearing in the text in bold, **like this**, are explained in the Glossary.

 Find out more about Australia at www.heinemannexplore.co.uk

Where is Australia?

To learn about Australia we meet three children who live there. Australia is a huge island. It is one of the biggest countries in the world.

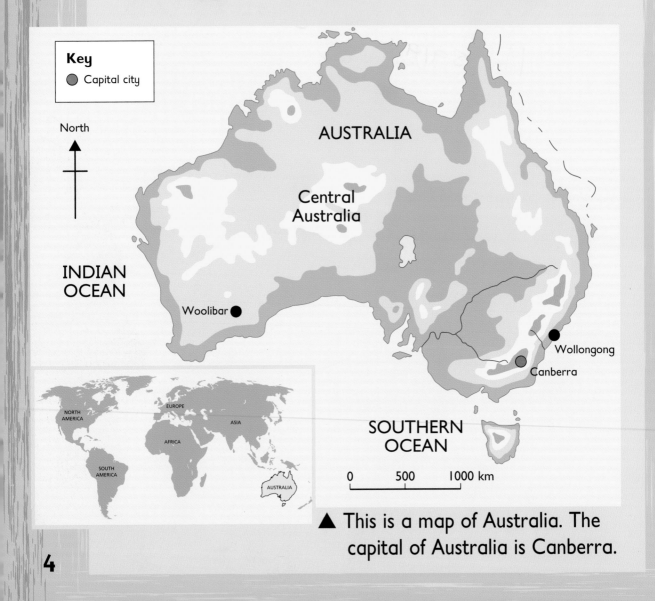

Key
- Capital city

North

AUSTRALIA

Central Australia

INDIAN OCEAN

Woolibar ●

Wollongong ●

Canberra ●

NORTH AMERICA

EUROPE

ASIA

AFRICA

SOUTH AMERICA

AUSTRALIA

SOUTHERN OCEAN

0   500   1000 km

▲ This is a map of Australia. The capital of Australia is Canberra.

Most of Australia is flat, hot **desert**. Many people live on the **coast**, where it is cooler. In the north, there is a large **rainforest**.

▲ Uluru is a big rock at the centre of Australia.

Meet Carly

Carly is seven years old. She lives with her parents and older sister, Emma. They live in a city called Wollongong.

Carly's mother

Carly's father

Emma

Carly

▲ This is Carly and her family in front of their house.

Wollongong is on the south-east coast of Australia. There are lots of sandy beaches here.

▲ Carly loves swimming in the sea.

At school

Carly's school is by the sea. She goes there on weekdays. School is from quarter to nine until quarter to three.

Hannah

▲ This is Carly and her best friend, Hannah, outside their school.

There are 32 children in Carly's class.
Their classroom is big and bright.
Carly and Hannah like learning on
the school computers.

Fun in the sun

After school, Carly does her homework. Then she likes to be outside. She is learning to play tennis.

At weekends, Carly's family spend time in the garden. They like cooking on their **barbecue**. They often invite friends over.

Sport

Many Australians enjoy playing or watching sport. Carly's sister and her friends go jogging to keep fit.

Lots of people play sport on the beach. It is fun to join a game of volleyball or try surfing.

Meet Georgia

Georgia is ten years old. Her family run a sheep farm in west Australia. She lives with her parents, her older sister, and the farm workers.

Georgia's father

farm worker

Georgia's mother

Georgia's sister

Georgia

The sheep farm lies on **grassland** near the **desert**. It covers a very large area. The nearest town is a long way away by car.

Down on the farm

There are lots of jobs to do on the sheep farm. Georgia helps out. She wants to be a farmer like her parents.

▲ Georgia is helping her father fix a fence.

Georgia looks after some of the horses on the farm. She rides a horse to help round up the sheep. Sometimes she uses a motorbike.

Living far away

Georgia lives too far from town to go to school. She has lessons over the radio and the Internet. Once a year, Georgia goes to a holiday camp to meet her classmates.

▲ Georgia's teacher talks to her over the radio.

Georgia's home is also a long way from a doctor or hospital. In an emergency the family call the Flying Doctor.

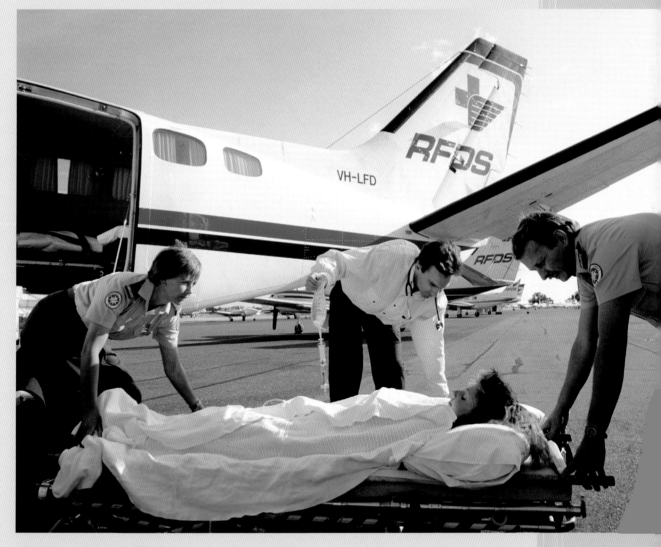

▲ The Flying Doctor comes to see Georgia's family in an aeroplane.

Australia's history

White people have only lived in Australia for about 250 years. People arrived from Britain first. **Settlers** from other countries made their homes there too.

▲ This is a Turkish restaurant in the town of Alice Springs.

When white people settled in Australia, they took the land from the people who already lived there. These people are known as **Aboriginals**.

▲ Today, some Aboriginal people are being given their land back.

Meet Dylan

Dylan is nine years old. He lives with his mother, father and younger sister, Natalia. His older brothers, Clifford and Dwayne, live near by.

Dylan's father

Dwayne

Clifford

Dylan

Dylan's mother

▲ Dylan's father is the local police officer.

Dylan's family are from an **Aboriginal tribe**. They live in a **desert** town in central Australia. Dylan's home is a **bungalow** with a large garden.

At work and play

Dylan's school starts at eight o'clock. He has lessons in English, maths, geography and **Aboriginal** studies.

After school, Dylan has jobs to do. He helps by washing up, watering the garden, and cleaning the car. Then he can play outside.

▲ Dylan likes splashing about with his friends at the local pool.

Life in the desert

The hot, red **desert** around Dylan's home is dry and dangerous. It is easy to get lost and run out of water.

▲ **Aboriginals** treat nature with great care.

Aboriginals know a lot about the land. Dylan and his friends often take trips into the desert because they know how to find water and things to eat.

◀ Dylan finds a type of banana in the desert.

Out and about in Australia

Australia has lots of special wildlife, such as koalas, kangaroos, and emus. There are many dangerous animals, like crocodiles, snakes and poisonous spiders.

The world's biggest area of **coral** is
in the ocean off Australia. It is called
the Great Barrier Reef. Divers go
there to watch sea creatures and
explore shipwrecks.

Australian fact file

Flag	Capital city	Money

	Canberra	Australian dollar

Religion
- Many white Australians are Christian. There are also Buddhists, Muslims and Jews. **Aboriginal** Australians have their own special beliefs.

Language
- The main language used in Australia today is English. There are 20 to 50 Aboriginal languages used too.

Try speaking Anangu Aboriginal!
These Anangu Aboriginal words are written the way they sound:

pahl-yah .... *hello, bye, good, OK*
oo-wah .... *yes*
kah-pee .... *water*

 Find out more about Australia at
www.heinemannexplore.co.uk

Glossary

Aboriginal people who first lived in Australia

barbecue type of grill for cooking food outside

bungalow house on just one level, without any rooms upstairs

coast where the land meets the sea

coral hard rock made of the shells of tiny dead sea creatures

desert very hot, dry area of land that has almost no rain and very few plants

grassland area of land that is mostly grass

rainforest thick forest of tall trees that grows in a hot, rainy place

settler person who comes to live in a country

tribe group of people who live closely together, sharing a language and beliefs

More books to read

Australia and Oceania, Mary Virginia Fox (Heinemann Library, 2002)

Around the World: Food, Margaret Hall (Heinemann Library, 2002)

Habitat Explorer: Desert Explorer, Greg Pyers (Raintree, 2004)

Index

Titles in the *We're From* series include:

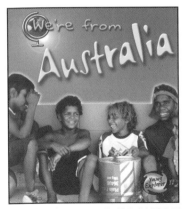

Hardback 0 431 11935 X

Hardback 0 431 11932 5

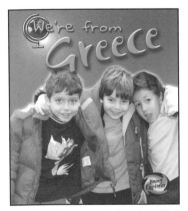

Hardback 0 431 11937 6

Hardback 0 431 11933 3

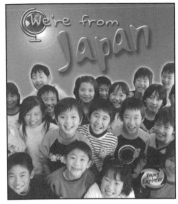

Hardback 0 431 11936 8

Hardback 0 431 11934 1

Find out about the other titles in this series on our website www.heinemann.co.uk/library